Gardening for Beginners

How to Design and Build an Inexpensive System for Growing Plants

Table of Contents

How to Design and Build an Inexpensive System for Growing Plants 1

Table of Contents 2

Quality matters 35

The cheaper the better 36

Getting the ground ready 39

Time to plant 41

Keeping your garden in good shape 43

Maintain and enjoy 49

Flowers 57

Natural dyes and paints 59

Potpourri 61

Crafts 62

Edibles and tea 64

Medicinal purposes 66

To blanket or not to blanket... 73

Seeds 88

Garden tools 89

Mulch 89

Potting soil 89

Compost and fertilizer 90

Local help and information 92

What's the Big Deal About Gardening?

Gardening is cheaper than therapy and you get tomatoes.

~Author Unknown

Most people like the idea of having a garden of some sort. I mean, who doesn't see the beauty in a colorful display of flowers, an array of pots filled with pretty posies (I thought the three p's would be fun) or interesting succulents, garden rows (long or short) ready to provide you with fresh veggies, or even a container or two of tomato plants, lettuce, or herbs for your culinary enjoyment? See? You're already envisioning what that might look like in your yard or on your patio.

Gardening has quite literally been around since the beginning of time. It's just one of those things that we are drawn to—either to do it, to admire it, or both. But why? Why is having a garden of some sort—even if it's nothing more than a few pots—such a big deal?

The answer depends on who you ask. That's because there are many reasons gardening is a 'big deal.' So let's look at the most popular reasons people like to garden to help you decide what kind of garden you should have, how big or small it should be, what you can expect to get out of gardening, or if it really is something you want to try your hand at.

Did I really just say you might decide gardening isn't for you? Yes, because it's true. There are some people who should not have a garden. They shouldn't even be trusted with a potted plant. Who are these people? If you agree with two or more of the following statements, I'm going to suggest you do one of two things: 1) stick with houseplants or 2) pass this book on to someone who can benefit from it.

- I do NOT enjoy going outside.

- I live in an apartment with little or no
- deck or patio space.

- I am rarely home and that's the way I like
- it.

My allergies are so bad I sneeze when I see pictures of flowers.

My idea of getting back to nature is wearing 100% cotton.

- I don't like vegetables and you can't
- make me.

I got a pet fish once, but that was last year, and I still haven't gotten around to getting fish food.

Okay, if you're still reading it's safe to assume you're ready to move forward in your gardening adventure and discover what the hype is all about. I hope so, because I'm excited to tell you and help you get started.

Gardening is good therapy. There are a number of therapeutic aspects to gardening. The quietness of working among the flowers and/or vegetables is proven to slow our breathing and help us relax both mentally and physically. Quiet time in the garden also allows us to restructure our thoughts and work things out in our minds. It's hard to stay mad or feel like there's nothing right in your world when you are surrounded by the sight and smell of flowers and/or knowing that before long you'll be eating the things you've helped grow.

Another possible therapeutic aspect of gardening is that it can help you release some pent-up frustration and stress. For example, a friend of mine takes a great deal of pleasure in cutting the corn stalks in one of her large gardens after the corn has been harvested. She covets this job each year. It's one of those things that makes momma happy. And you know what they say about if momma ain't happy... 😊

Gardening provides a sense of accomplishment. Does this even need an explanation? How can you not get a confidence boost when you see little seedlings popping up through the soil and then watch those seedlings get another set of leaves, then another, until they become everything they're is supposed to be? Sitting down to eat a meal you've prepared with the tomatoes, green beans, lettuce, or whatever else you might have grown is priceless.

Gardening is a great way to get in shape and stay healthy. Bending, standing, hoeing, raking, pulling weeds, deadheading flowers, carrying a water can and dragging a hose around is exercise. No, you're not going to burn off enough calories to eat a giant piece of chocolate cake every day, but it's great cardio that will keep your heart rate up and burn more fat than you would by sitting around all day.

The vitamin D you derive from soaking up some sunshine is great for your health, too. There is a catch to this, though. Your chances of absorbing vitamin D from the sun are drastically reduced when you wear sunscreen with an SPF over 8. This leaves you wondering which is better—the vitamin D or protection from the sun. The answer is both. While you shouldn't prolong your exposure to the sun without some form of protection, the sun's rays are one of the few natural sources of vitamin D. Vitamin D is essential for strong, healthy bones, the formation of blood cells, and strengthening the immune system. It can also help absorb phosphorus and calcium, and is often used to help people recover from or fight off certain diseases and illnesses, such as rickets, eczema, psoriasis and jaundice.

PLEASE NOTE: By mentioning that exposure to the sun can be good for you, I am in no way trying to hand out medical advice. I am simply stating the facts regarding the benefits of vitamin D and that the sun is the best source of it. Please do not use what I have said as your permission slip to toss the sunscreen in the trash. Just be reasonable and remember that none of us are vampires. We can enjoy limited exposure to the sun without fear of deathly consequences.

Gardening teaches responsibility. All kids need chores. All adults need chores, too— things that we are solely responsible for getting done. Things that if not done properly, will have negative outcomes. We need these chores so that we can learn to be responsible. So that we can witness first-hand what it means to see something to completion. So that we can feel accomplished and so that we can make a positive contribution to our existence. None of us should be content with just being here. We need to *want* to make our world a better place.

If you give children the responsibility of weeding, watering, and deadheading flowers—either in a flower garden or in pots—not only will they learn to be responsible, they will learn about the process of how things grow and what it takes to keep things growing at optimal levels. They will (or should) also learn what happens when they act responsibly... or not, i.e. earning an allowance, having flowers or vegetables to enjoy and/or sell, learning to use what they grow in different ways, etc.

We adults need to be reminded of the importance of responsibility, too. Often times we get so wrapped up in what we want and what we think we need, that we become a bit selfish. Having a garden that depends on us for its health, beauty, and success keeps us humble and grounded (no pun intended... okay, maybe just a little bit intended).

Gardening teaches simple facts of life we should already know, but sometimes don't. I have to share something with you here—

something that sounds funny, but really isn't. Darcy, a young military wife who had been raised on a farm in mid-Missouri, was living on the coast of California, enjoying all the fresh produce available in a place with a much longer growing season. One day, while she was strolling up and down the rows at a farmer's market, she stopped to buy some new potatoes, squash, and cumquats. As she stood admiring all the things the couple behind the table had grown, another young woman and her preschool-aged daughter made their way to the table.

The little girl noticed the huge heads of broccoli and asked her mom what they were. The mom replied, "Broccoli… I think." The little girl then asked, "Where does broccoli come from?" The mom looked at her like she was completely ignorant and said, "It comes from… from… broccoli!" Not satisfied, the little girl asked, "But how does it get to be broccoli?" The exasperated mom huffed back to her little girl, "I don't know, and I don't care!"

Unable to keep quiet any longer, Darcy smiled at the girl and said, "Broccoli grows from seeds. It's a plant that farmers grow in their gardens so we can eat it." The couple whose stand it was told the girl that was right, and then offered to let her try a bite.

She smiled a big, shy smile as a thank-you to Darcy. The little girl's mom, however, shot Darcy a look that was nothing short of disgust. How dare she tell her child where broccoli comes from?

The point of this sad, funny, and true story is that we need to know the basics of how things grow and where our food comes from. It makes us more appreciative and respectful.

Gardening can save money. Most people I know don't regularly purchase fresh-cut flowers to enjoy. It's just one of those things we don't bother with. Unless, that is, you are the type of person who is conscientious about supporting local growers by buying them from a farmer's market. But if you grow your own, you can save money *and* have flowers all throughout your growing season.

Growing your own vegetables saves money too. Yes, you will have the initial investment of jars and other equipment for canning, or durable freezer containers, but those things can be used time and again, so once you have them, you have them. Some people might try to tell you that by the time you water the garden, keep it weeded, and take the time to harvest what you grow, you are not saving any money, but if you garden efficiently, that's simply not true. And even if it were a break-even venture, the quality of the produce you grow is ALWAYS going to be better because the nutrients won't have been cooked away or preserved with an overload of salt.

Gardening is fun. 'Nuff said.

Before we go any further, we need to make sure you are familiar with the most commonly used gardening terms. I hope this doesn't seem too juvenile or 'dumbed down' for you. If so, I apologize, but I'd rather do that than leave you asking, "What is he talking about?"

Aeration: Aeration is a word that simply means 'to add air' to something. In this case, that 'something' is the soil for your flower or vegetable garden. Soil that is compacted by constant or heavy foot-traffic, large root systems, or even too much pounding rain, needs to be aerated. This means it needs to be loosened up so the air (oxygen) can flow through it. Why? Because the soil needs oxygen in order to produce the organisms that plants need to feed off of.

Annual: A plant that has a lifecycle of one year or one growing season

Bulb: The round part of the stem in some flowers or plants that grows underground and is capable of growing a new plant. Example: tulip, daffodil, onion

Companion planting: Planting different types of plants together so that both (or all) can benefit from being next to one another

Compost: Rotted and decaying plant or other organic matter that can be used to fertilize and nourish the soil

Deadhead: Removal of dead (spent) blooms from flowers, which will enable the plant to produce more flowers

Dormant: A plant that is alive, but not actively growing

Fertilizer: Plant and soil food/nutrients

Germination: The point at which a seed begins to grow

Hardening off: Introducing plants that have been started indoors (or in a greenhouse) to the outdoors. This is also done with houseplants that are brought in each winter and placed outside in the spring.

Heirloom: Plants (usually vegetables) that are reproduced through natural or open pollination. Heirloom plant seeds reproduce the same kind of plant. Example: Yellow Pear tomatoes and Top Crop bush-style green beans are heirloom varieties.

Hybrid: A plant that has been produced by carefully and deliberately cross-pollinating two different varieties of the same plant. Planting hybrid seeds will not yield the same results as the plant from which it came. Example: Early Girl tomatoes are hybrid, as is Peaches and Cream corn.

Perennial: A plant that lies dormant through the winter but begins a new lifecycle with each new growing season

Ph level: The amount of acid in the soil

Planting zone: A designated area for growing based on the average growing season (length of growing season, average high and low

temperatures, average first and last frost dates)

Pollination: Fertilization of a flower, fruit, or vegetable. Pollination happens as a result of wind, insects, and birds, and can be done artificially by people. The male pollen is joined with the female stigma to form a seed. The seed is usually surrounded by either the blooms of a flower or a fruit or vegetable. Example: zinnias, apples, peppers

Propagate: Multiplying or breeding plants by one of the following methods: sewing seed, root division, bulb division, or stem cuttings

Prune: Cutting back excess growth of a plant in order to reshape it, control its growth, and concentrate its nutrients where they are needed most

Rootbound: A root ball that is compacted in its container, prohibiting proper growth and nutrient distribution

Seedling: A seed that has developed two sets of leaves

Self-seeding: Plants that drop their seeds onto the soil during the growing season, leaving the seeds to stay dormant in the ground until the following year. The seeds that come up are known as 'volunteers.'

Thinning: Removing excess seedlings so that the plants are not too crowded and to allow a few plants to get proper nutrition so that they will grow full and lush

Tuber: The thick part of the stem or rhizome of a plant that is capable of forming another plant NOTE: A rhizome is the lower part of the stem of some plants that grows horizontally to the ground and is capable of growing another plant. Example: Iris

THREE
Garden Strategy

No matter where you are you can grow something to eat. Shift your thinking and you'd be surprised at the places your food can be

grown! Windowsill, fire escape and rooftop gardens have the same potential to provide impressive harvests as backyard gardens, greenhouses and community spaces. ~Greg Peterson

Now that you've decided you are going to have a garden, it's time for you to decide what kind of garden you want and what you want to grow.

CAUTION: It is easy to get so excited about planting your garden that you want to grow more than you have time to care for or room to plant. That's why I recommend you start small-ish and work up from there, depending on your experience, the amount of space you have available, and the time you have to devote to your garden.

REMEMBER: It is better to have a small garden that is well-cared for and producing its full bounty, than to have a large garden in need of attention you can't give it.

To help you decide what kind of garden you should have, let's look at the various types of gardens. We'll explore the pros and cons of each, along with the requirements necessary for their success. After you've had a chance to think about everything you are about to learn, you will be able to decide which type(s) of gardening you are best suited for.

Traditional flower beds. Traditional flower beds are homes to flowers planted directly into the ground. They can be home to perennials and annuals grown from seed and/or seedlings and plants that have been separated to form new plants. Traditional flower beds can be any size or shape and usually have defined boundaries. These boundaries are usually 'marked' or designated with rocks, mulch, landscape timbers, or some other sort of intentional border. Traditional flower beds can be laid out any way you wish. There is no set way plants should be placed in the flower bed other than making sure the taller plants don't overshadow the smaller ones, which makes it difficult to see everything you've planted.

The pros and cons of traditional flower beds include:

- As long as you make sure the soil is nutrient-rich, you can have a flowerbed just about anywhere.

- Plants that are native to a particular area, as well as a large number of hardy perennials or annuals, will grow well in a traditional flower bed with minimal input on your part.

- Traditional flower beds require you to remove the sod (grass), remove rocks, and till the soil several times over before planting. This means it takes more time and effort to properly prepare than raised beds.

- Traditional beds are suitable for flowering shrubs, ornamental grasses, and all other types of plants without the risk of them becoming rootbound.

- Traditional beds allow for easy self-seeding and self-propagation without worrying about plants becoming overcrowded or rootbound.

- People tend to plan bigger gardens when they go the traditional route vs. raised beds or container gardens. This isn't a 'con' unless you plant more than you can take care of.

Traditional vegetable garden. Traditional vegetable gardens are those in which seeds or seedlings are sown directly into the ground. Vegetable gardens can be any size and shape, but the size of the garden is more important when determining what you can grow than it is with a flower bed. Vegetable gardens are best planted in rows, with some vegetables needing a lot more space than others. Companion planting should also be taken into consideration when planting vegetables.

Traditional vegetable gardens come with more pros than cons:

- Traditional gardens are best for growing things like corn, melons, and root crops (potatoes, carrots, sweet potatoes, and onions).

- Traditional vegetable gardens tend to do better than smaller raised beds or container vegetables because vegetables tend to need more room than flowers.

- The bigger the garden, the more room there is for weeds to grow.
- Once the plants are big enough to bear their produce, it is usually not possible to till between the rows, making it more labor-intensive to

keep the garden weed-free.

Raised beds. Raised beds are flower beds or vegetable

a contained or boxed area usually 8 to 10 inches above ground level. The soil in a raised bed has been built up with peat moss and compost to make it high in nutrients. NOTE: You can (and should) build your soil in this way no matter what kind of garden/beds you have.

Raised beds are generally small (8 to 16 feet long and wide). They are typically easier to maintain and manage. Additionally:

- Raised beds are relatively easy to prepare. All you have to do is build your bottomless box(es), fill with quality gardening soil, and plant.

- Raised beds are easy to maintain and control; you can put the best possible soil in your beds to promote optimal growth.

- Raised beds are easy to build and don't have to cost a lot of money. You can build them from tubs you cut the bottoms out of, landscape timbers, treated lumber, synthetic 'lumber,' or even large rocks or bricks.

Container gardens. A container garden actually consists of a lot of individual gardens, with each plant having its own pot to grow in. Or in some cases, a large pot can be used to grow a variety of herbs or greens. Container gardens obviously require the least amount of space and are easiest to keep weeded but require more care in making sure they receive the right amount of water. You are also much more limited in what you can grow in a container garden.

Container gardens work for most types of flowers, but some will have to be pot-friendly varieties. For example, traditional 'giant' zinnias don't do well in pots (unless they are REALLY big), but the smaller varieties (lily-put and minis) and even the mid-size do fine. The same holds true for ornamental grasses. Growing them in pots requires a LARGE pot.

Additionally:

- Container gardens can be expensive. Pots large enough to grow tomatoes and peppers (among other veggies) and flowers of any kind are pretty pricey.

• Containers don't have enough soil in them to store up water and nutrients in the soil.

Container gardens are better for flowers and herbs than vegetables.

• Container gardens are the only option
• you have if you live in an apartment, on the water (houseboat), or in a place where you are not allowed to dig in the yard.

Hothouse gardening. Growing flowers and/or vegetables in a controlled environment that simulates an optimal growing season. Hothouse gardening is done in a greenhouse using raised beds and containers.

Few people garden using a hothouse or greenhouse due to the expense of maintaining the structure. This method of gardening is usually reserved for commercial growers.

Non-traditional gardening methods. Straw bale gardening, vertical gardening, and hydroponic gardening are the three most widely known methods of non-traditional gardening.

Straw bale gardening is exactly what it sounds like. You plant your seeds or seedlings in bales of straw you line up in rows and then tend to it like you would any other garden, i.e. water, feed, and so forth. Straw gardening has proven to be productive, easy, and a fairly low maintenance means of growing fresh vegetables. Most people don't resort to straw bale gardening for flowers, though, as it is not very attractive, and the purpose of growing flowers is to add beauty to your landscape.

When using straw bales to raise vegetables, keep the following in mind:

- The bales are not dense enough to raise things like corn, okra, and root crops (potatoes, onions).

- The bales break down over time; you need to make sure your tomatoes have proper support.

- Arranging a platform of straw bales can keep cucumbers, pumpkins, squash, and melons off the ground.

- Too much water can cause the bales to get moldy, so watch your plants for signs of mold.

- If it is hot and dry, you will have to water the bales more often, as they don't usually retain much water unless left out in soaking rains.

- It's somewhat easy to keep the bales weeded.

Vertical gardening includes:

- 'Training' plants that vine (cucumbers, pumpkins, melons) to grow up onto a trellis instead of on the ground.

- Using a ladder-type frame to hold small raised beds instead of having them on the ground.

- Growing small items like herbs and greens in upright pallets or racks.

Vertical gardening using trellises has been around for centuries. In fact, pole-style green beans are climbers, meaning they climb a fence or trellis instead of bushing out like the beans you likely are familiar with. Using trellises to restrict the area where your vining crops grow is wise and makes them much more manageable. Other points to consider when deciding whether vertical gardening is for you:

- Vertical raised beds will need to be much smaller than flat raised beds.

- You are severely limited on what you can grow due to weight and root depth needs of most vegetables.

Because the garden is off the ground, it is
- easier to keep weed-free.

- The smaller containers mean more frequent watering is required.

Now let's look at vertical gardening from a flower standpoint. There are a number of beautiful flowers that can be grown in a vertical garden structure. Most of them are annuals such as marigolds, petunias, begonias, rose moss (portulaca), alyssum, and other small, slightly compact plants. Succulents are another great option for this kind of setup. They are low-maintenance and easy to keep in small containers.

Vertical flower gardens can serve as backdrops for ground level gardens, they can hide things you don't want spoiling your landscape (AC units, trash bins, or the compost bin), and they can even create a wall along the deck or patio.

Hydroponic gardening is the process of gardening using water enriched with nutrients instead of soil. Proponents and hobbyists of hydroponic gardening have grown a wide variety of herbs, vegetables, and houseplants using this system, but they can only use this system of gardening with seedling plants... grown in soil.

If this is something you think you would like to try, by all means do so. I will warn you, however, that setting up a hydroponic garden system is not cheap and requires a lot of care and maintenance.

Choosing the right method of gardening for YOU is what will make your gardening adventure a positive and rewarding experience. So how do you choose which one is right for you?

- Decide what your motive is for gardening. Do you want to try something new? Do you want to grow your hobby into something more than it currently is? Do you want to grow some of your own food? Do you want your children to learn how their food is grown? Do you want to give your children something to be responsible for and create a shared activity to enjoy with them? Do you simply want to make your landscape more aesthetic and have an excuse to spend more time outside?

- Decide how much space you are willing to care for. A well maintained garden of any kind is the only kind of garden to have. Taking on more than you can reasonably keep up with is the same as setting yourself up to fail. A plain yard is better than a yard with unkempt flower and vegetable gardens.

- Decide what to grow. This is a matter of personal taste with a bit of growing zone practicality thrown in for good measure.

- Consider your budget. Plants can get expensive, so start with the easy and inexpensive varieties. Don't sink a lot of money into flowering bushes and exotic plants until you know you will take the time and effort to care them for properly.

- Consider your resources. Do you have an outdoor hydrant? You can't very well have a vegetable garden without one. It would be inefficient and exhausting to have to carry water from indoors. You also need to take into consideration the placement of your garden in respect to where your outdoor hydrant is located. The closer, the better.

Whichever method you choose, gardening can bring you a great deal of enjoyment, satisfaction, and relaxation. The key to making sure that's what you get from your gardening experience is in choosing the right kind of garden for YOU.

FOUR

Garden Must-Haves

Essential advice for the gardener: grow peas of mind, lettuce be thankful, squash selfishness, turnip to help thy neighbor, and always make thyme for loved ones. ~Author Unknown

No matter what you're doing—be it a job or a hobby—there are always a few essentials necessary for doing it right. It would even be fair to say that the success of a job or hobby often hinges on whether or not the person has the essential items to work with. For example, I recall watching one of those made-for-television movies several years ago, about a teacher who took on the challenge of teaching in a small one-room school in a poverty-stricken mining town. The kids were way behind academically, but it wasn't because they were incapable of learning. It was because they didn't have textbooks or other learning resources that were current and grade appropriate. Being the feel-good movie it was, the teacher went above and beyond to find funding for what the students needed and they all lived happily ever after.

It was a good movie, but more than that, it illustrated just how important it is to have the right tools for the job—no matter what that job is. On the flipside, sometimes we have difficulty discerning between needs and wants or luxuries. An example of this is the humble garden trowel. A garden trowel is a miniature hand-held shovel. It is an absolute essential for any gardener. But as you can imagine, there are countless brands available in different price ranges. The most basic, durable trowels made by respected and trustworthy companies run in the $5 to $10 range. Then there are the fancier trowels. For example, I saw one that was white with little pink roses all over it. It cost $14 and was not made from the same durable metals as many of the others.

Do you see the difference between necessity and luxury?

So now I'll give you a simple list of necessities for a successful gardening experience. You might not need each of these items. For example, if you are going to use a raised bed system, you won't need a garden tiller. A garden weasel will be sufficient.

I want to stress that sometimes, the cheaper the better, but other times, spending a bit more for a quality item is worth it. I've categorized the items into these two groups.

Quality matters

- Hoe, rakes (garden and leaf), shovels (spade and sharpshooter)

- Garden hose

- Hand trowel

- Garden weasel or tiller (The size of the tiller depends on the size of the garden, so the bigger the garden, the higher quality tiller you need.)

- Wheelbarrow

-

- Tomat

o

cages

and

trellise

s

Garde

n   or

pottin

g soil

The cheaper the better

- Watering can (You can use an empty and well-rinsed milk jug.)

- Garden gloves

- Seeds and plants (as long as the seeds aren't expired or the plants aren't brown and half-dead)

- Sprinkler (This one is iffy when it comes to quality vs. cheap, so why not compromise with a mid-priced version? The important thing is that it has the radius you need and will stay upright.)

- Compost bucket/container

- Shears (An old pair of scissors often
- works just fine.)

Garden sprays (Blue DAWN dish soap and water in a mister bottle is top-notch.)

•Misc. handheld garden tools (bulb planter, claw, dandelion puller)

You can purchase your tools at garden centers, warehouse stores, or big box discount stores. Another great place to find some quality garden tools is a farm auction or moving sale. You might end up paying more than you should at one of these, but the quality of the older items you'll find there is usually far superior to that of newer versions.

NOTE: When buying used garden tools, make sure the handles are secure and tight on things like rakes and shovels, that the fittings and gaskets on a hose are in good shape, and that there are no breaks or splits in the hose itself. A wheelbarrow's tire should be aired up, the handles should be solid, and the body of the wheelbarrow should be firmly attached to the frame. If you buy a used tiller, ask to operate it for a few minutes to make sure the tines are sharp

SHOVEL
FIVE
Let's Do This!

Why try to explain miracles to your kids when you can just have them plant a garden? ~ Robert Brault

You know you want to have a garden. ☐

You know what kind of garden(s) you want to have. ☐

You know what you want to grow in your garden(s). ☐

Now it's time to put the shovel to the sod and get to work on making your gardening dreams a reality.

Getting the ground ready

The first thing you have to do is prepare the ground for becoming a garden. Or if you are building raised beds, you will need to build your frames and get them filled.

To prepare the ground that will become your garden space, you must do the following:

- Remove the sod. This is usually done by 'cutting' it. This is done with a straight-edged shovel or sharpshooter shovel, cutting down an inch or two into the soil, just enough to get the sod (grass) out of the ground. Think of it as scalping the ground. Most people cut the sod off in square sections or short rows. You can then place the sod in other areas of your yard to help fill in bare spaces in the lawn. Simply lay the pieces of sod on the ground, tamp them down lightly by stepping on them a few times, and give them a nice drink of water. You will need to keep them moist (not wet) for a few days so they can 'take' to the new ground.

- After you remove the sod, use a garden rake to rough up the dirt to get roots from the grass that were left behind and any rocks that were hiding beneath the surface. After you rake it to the edge, put it in a lawn waste container.
- Using a tiller or shovel (depending on the size of your garden), turn the dirt over 6 to 10 inches deep. A tiller will break the ground up more uniformly than a shovel.

- If you use a shovel, you will need to go over what you've done with a hoe to break the soil down even more. The purpose of this is to:

- Loosen the soil so you can mix in the peat moss, manure, and/or compost so that the soil will be able to provide more nutrients to your plants.

- Loosen the soil, making it easier for seedlings to break through and for tender root systems to grab hold of the soil and plant themselves.

- Loosen the soil to aid in water absorption.

Time to plant

Once the soil is ready for planting, you can start... planting.

- If you are planting flowers, you can now sow the seeds or put the plants in the ground. When placing your plants or sowing your seeds, there isn't any right or wrong way to design or lay out the scheme of your flowerbed—other than to be conscious of the various heights of full-grown plants. You don't want your dianthus to be hidden by the cone flowers, do you?

- If you are planting a vegetable garden, you will need to plant in rows. To make your rows, use the hoe to mound the dirt up in rows, making mounds 4 to 6 inches tall. It is also a good idea to lightly pack the rows so that they don't collapse the first time it rains or you water it with the hose or sprinkler. NOTE: Planting your seeds or seedlings in raised rows makes it easier for you to distinguish your rows and keep them weeded, prevents the rows from getting too packed down, helps with drainage so that young plants don't get drowned in a heavy rain or watering session, and looks tidy and neat.

- Like I said earlier, companion planting is a real thing, so pay attention to the what and why of the companion planting chart included in this chapter.

- Pay attention to spacing and depth instructions on seed packets and plant markers.

- Pay attention to planting zones when thinking about perennials you want to include.

- Pay attention to the sun or shade requirements and make sure the plants you want to include will get the proper amount of sun or shade.

After planting your plants or seeds, give them a big (but not too big) drink of water. Make sure you don't dump water on your seeds and young plants. Dumping water on seeds will wash them to the surface and displace them. Dumping water on young plants can damage them and break them down. Watering cans have a sprinkling effect for a reason. The gentle shower of water is what the plants need. You can create this same effect from a hand-held sprinkler attachment for your garden hose. Most hand-held sprinkler wands also have a pressure adjustment valve that will enable you to control the pressure of the water hitting the ground and your plants.

Keeping your garden in good shape

Now it's time to sit back and watch them grow. Well, sort of. You won't have much to do for the first couple of weeks, but you need to check on your garden daily. As the seeds start popping through the ground, you will need to carefully thin out some of the tiny seedlings.

Thinning out your plants (if necessary) is the process of removing some of them (either throwing them away or transplanting them somewhere else) so that you will have a few strong, healthy, vibrant plants instead of a lot of not-so-healthy ones. You need to be very careful when thinning out your plants, as you want to cause as little disruption to the seedlings as possible. It is best to use your fingers or tweezers to thin your plants.

You also need to check your plants and seedlings every day or two to make sure nothing is eating them. Rabbits, slugs, bugs, and deer are just a few possible culprits. You can guard against critter attacks by spraying or dusting your plants with SEVIN or with a solution of blue DAWN dish soap and water. You can also plant marigolds around the perimeter of your vegetable garden and in and among your flower beds. Marigolds, along with zinnias, lavender, and sage, are all good for keeping the rabbits away. Since the little bunny rabbits like to hop in and munch on lettuce, strawberries, the tops of green beans, and just about anything else they can reach, you would do well to plant a border of deterring flowers around these plants.

As for flowerbeds, rabbits are also not too keen on Shasta daisies and coneflowers, so make sure you have a few in and among the flowers they do like (iris, petunias, and tulips).

Don't underestimate the power of a dollar store pie tin (or two or three). Attach them to stakes sporadically throughout the garden to scare off rabbits and other wildlife. OR if you don't want to ruin the aesthetic of your garden (and I don't blame you), invest in a few ceramic or resin animals that are lifesize (or nearly so). Cats, dogs, owls, and chickens scare critters away.

Scattering mothballs around the edge of perimeter of your garden and flowerbeds also keeps the rabbits away. Just be sure you don't do this if you have a pet or young child who might ingest them.

Deer are not too keen on chives, garlic, cosmos, daffodils, peonies, or lavender. They do, however, enjoy munching on hostas, daylilies, tomatoes, corn, and beans. You can often keep deer away from the plants they enjoy by planting things they don't like around the perimeter of your flowerbeds. As for your vegetable garden, since most of the plants deer don't like are perennials, which are inconvenient to have in your vegetable garden, I highly recommend using any or all of the following:

- Coarsely shave a few bars of strongly scented soap and scatter it around the perimeter and up and down the rows of your garden. Deer don't like the sweet scents we do. They find them unappealing.

- You can use dryer sheets, although they tend to blow away. A scarecrow or ceramic or resin dog can keep the deer at bay, too.

- Human hair. If you have a beautician friend who will let you sweep their floor (no joke), scattering the hair around the garden keeps the deer away.

Slugs are a nuisance and should be dealt with as soon as you notice them. And by notice them, I mean you need to be looking for them—especially if you live in a wet climate or have a definite rainy season. Slugs love dark, damp environments—especially moist soil filled with fruits, veggies, and lots of yummy green leaves. They are also especially fond of hostas.

Slugs come out at night, so the best time to find them is early in the morning, or if you are really dedicated, with a flashlight at night. But don't feel like you need to do that. It's not necessary—especially if you set some traps for them:

- Bury a few plastic cups in your garden, leaving ½ to 1 inch above the ground. Fill the cup halfway full of beer or milk. In the morning, dispose of the liquid and the slugs that drowned in it overnight.

- Turn a few pint-sized canning jars on their side and place 2 tablespoons of cornmeal in them (about midway in the jar). The next morning you will likely have dead slugs in or around the jar, as they go into the jar to eat the meal and it swells up inside them and kills them.

• You can also deter the slugs by watering your plants in the morning instead of the evening. This gives the ground time to dry out a little before nightfall.

Bugs are a two-sided coin in the world of gardening. Some bugs, like cabbage worms, mites, mealybugs, and aphids (to name a few) are a nightmare in the garden. Other bugs, however, such as lady bugs, praying mantis, assassin bugs, some beetles, damsel bugs, and syrphid flies are a gardener's friend. They eat bad • bugs and their larvae. So, before you go on • a bug-killing rampage, get to know your good bugs from your bad bugs. Here are a few websites that will help you:

https://www.thoughtco.com/top-beneficial-garden-insects-1968404
https://www.organiclesson.com/beneficial-insects-garden-pestcontrol/

- http://www.birdsandblooms.com/gardening/garden-bugs/

Maintain and enjoy

Once your flowers start blooming and your vegetables start producing, there are two things you need to do:

ONE: Enjoy the fruits of your labor.

TWO: Maintain it so you can get the most out of it.

Seeing and smelling the flowers you've planted and/or enjoying the fresh food you grow are two of the most satisfying things a person can experience. But you can't do either of these things without maintaining what you started. Think of it as getting a puppy and spending a week trying to get it housebroken and then giving up. Or telling your kindergartner he or she is on their own—that you've done all you're going to do for them.

Maintaining your garden is one of those things that easily falls into the category of "a little bit goes a long way." What I mean is that doing a little bit every day or so goes a long way toward keeping our gardens in good shape. By spending thirty minutes to an hour a day (depending on how big your garden is) tending to your plants, vs. letting them go until they're in serious need of attention, you will save yourself from having to spend hours and hours trying to get everything back in good shape.

Garden maintenance includes:

Watering as needed. The following guidelines are just that—guidelines. It all comes down to a matter of common sense and paying attention to your plants. If the ground is hot and dry, the plants are going to look parched. Don't leave them like this for very long. Going from one extreme to another is hard on a plant. It stresses their system and affects their ability to perform at maximum capacity.

•Plants that are in the ground usually require the least amount of watering. Unless you are experiencing a drought or excessive heat, most flowers will do just fine with watering two or three times a week. Again, this depends on the amount of rainfall you have, the temperature, and the type of flowers you are growing.

• Some vegetables will require more water if there is little rainfall and high heat. Cucumbers, for example, need a lot more moisture than potatoes and onions.

• Flowers and vegetables in raised beds can usually be watered with the same • frequency as in-ground flowers and vegetables.

Container plants need water much more frequently. They can only hold so much at a time without becoming too wet, so you should never drench a plant in a pot. Water it until the soil is moist and stop. Unglazed ceramic pots are especially thirsty, as their porous composition soaks up the water—even wicking it away from the soil, where it is most needed.

As you will read later on, some plants need more water than others, so if having to water your plants frequently isn't something you want to have to do, you need to choose what to grow based on their low-maintenance factor rather than their eye-appeal.

Weeding is one of those things you must do whether you want to or not. One of the best ways to reduce the amount of weeding you will have to do, is to start with ground that is as weed-free as possible. Taking the time to get as many weeds out of the ground where your garden area will be is the best thing you can do for yourself and your plants. Aside from that, by spending a few minutes every other day weeding a few rows in the vegetable garden and a few minutes every other day pulling weeds from your flower beds, the task will never seem overwhelming.

Other ways you can cut down on the amount of weeding necessary include using ground cover under your flower beds and covering the surface with rock or mulch, laying ground cover between the rows of your vegetable garden, filling your beds with flowers, and planting something in nearly every inch of available soil in your vegetable garden. NOTE: The motive behind planting things so close together is to reduce the amount of space weeds can grow.

Some weeding will have to be done by hand—literally pulling the weeds from the ground with your hands. In larger spaces, you can hoe up the dirt all around the plants and then pick the loose weeds out and discard them.

Deadheading is essential for a pretty flower bed. You should get rid of wilted, dried up blooms daily. This will allow more nutrients from the plant to be used to make more blooms and healthier foliage. To deadhead, simply pull the dead flowers off the plant with your fingers or snip them off with a pair of garden scissors.

Spraying and fertilizing is another 'must.' Spraying for pests can be done periodically just for safety sake but is usually only done at the first sign of trouble. By keeping this aspect of garden maintenance to a minimum, you will be allowing nature to do its thing, i.e. letting the good bugs take care of the bad ones. There are exceptions, however, to this rule. For example, if you were around last year for the Japanese beetle explosion, you know spraying was about as common as watering. YIKES!

For those of you who are anti-chemical, you can use gentler concoctions such as the dish soap spray I've mentioned a few times. Cayenne pepper and water are effective in killing ants, orange oil mixed with water and dish soap kills slugs and roaches, and tobacco and water sprayed on plants kills aphids. For more natural recipes, you can search sites like Pinterest and get more information than you'll be able to process.

Fertilizing is something you can do for the soil and your plants. You should fertilize the soil every fall and spring by adding compost, manure, or commercial fertilizers to it. Fertilizing plants should be done carefully—not too often and not too heavily. Too much fertilizer 'burns' plants, meaning it is too strong. Overfertilizing can weaken and even kill a plant.

If your soil is well-fertilized, you won't need to fertilize your plants— especially if they are in the ground or in raised beds. Plants raised in pots, straw bales, or hydroponic gardens will need fertilizer. Liquid fertilizers or fertilizer sticks you bury in the soil are your best options. Just be sure to follow the directions on the package. Or, if you prefer to go a more natural

- route, you can do any of the following:

- Water your plants with fish emulsion mixed with water.

- Spread coffee grounds and/or finely crushed eggshells on the soil and mix it into the surface of the soil.

Bury chopped banana peels in your potted plants.

Water your plants with pure molasses water (1 tablespoon to a gallon of water), unsweet tea, or Epsom salts water (1 tablespoon to a gallon of water).

See! Caring for your garden is not all that difficult or time consuming. Unless you have large areas to care for, the average person can do all that needs to be done in the same amount of time it takes to watch one or two television shows. And it's better to tend to potatoes than to be a couch potato.

List of Common Garden Weeds

Dandelion

Purslane

Plantain

Quack Grass

Crab Grass

Saw Thistle

Carpet Weed

Chickweed

SIX

The Harvest

The garden is a love song, a duet between a human being and Mother Nature. ~Jeff Cox

How you harvest your garden, how much you harvest, and what you do with your harvest, depends (of course) on what you grow. Nothing mindboggling about that, is there? But it is something you need to think about during the planning stages. You need to think about what you want to do with what you grow—even if all you want to do is look at it. But almost every plant has at least one purpose beyond its good looks, so why not get the most out of your garden?

The tips and suggestions I'm going to give you in these next few pages are not by any means a complete list. Even my imagination and knowledge only go so far. But trust me—I'm going to give you plenty to choose from.

Flowers

The most common reason we harvest fresh flowers is to make bouquets to display and enjoy in our home. We also might give them to someone to express our love, cheer someone up, or comfort the sick or grieving.

Flowers most suitable for bouquets include:

- Roses
- Iris
- Sunflowers
- Lilies
- Daffodils
- Zinnias
- Lilacs
- Forsythia

Baby's breath
- Tulips
- Larkspur
- Peony
- Daisy
- Black-eyed Susan
- Ranunculus
- Mums
- Gladioli
- Yarrow

Carnations

Those not suitable for bouquets include:

Petunia
- Rose moss
- Dianthus (some varieties will work)
- Columbine
- Passion vine
- Geraniums
- Alyssum
- Begonia

Marigolds

Like I said earlier, flowers have a lot more to offer than just their pretty faces. Flowers can be used for:

Natural dyes and paints

Using plants and flowers to make your own dye is a lot of fun. You can use the dye to color fabrics (cotton fabrics work best) or paper, and to paint on wood or ceramics. The rule of thumb for making plant dyes is to chop the plant material, place it in a pot, add twice as much water as you have plant material, bring it to a boil, and then simmer on low heat for an hour. Remove it from the heat and let it set for an hour (or longer if you want more intense colors). Strain the plant material from the dye and ta-da... it is ready to use!

To dye fabric, you will need to 'fix' it by simmering it in a saltwater solution or vinegar and water solution for about an hour. Then squeeze and rinse it in cold water and squeeze out the excess water again before placing it in the dye. NOTE: Fixing the fabric helps the fibers absorb the dye so the color will be permanent.

Paper, wood, and ceramic don't have to go through the fixing process.

Here is a partial list of flowers and plants and the colors they create:

- Orange: Barberry, carrots, lilac twigs, (who would have thought) onion skins, sassafras leaves, sunflowers

- Brown: Acorns, coneflower leaves and stems, dandelion roots, geraniums, pine bark, walnut hulls

- Pink: Avocado skins, cherries, dandelion blooms, roses, lavender, strawberries

- Blue or Purple: Blueberries, blackberries, coneflower petals, grapes, red cabbage, purple iris, Queen Ann's lace

- Red: Beets, sumac berries, dried red geraniums, basil, dried rose moss flowers (mixed with salt), raspberries

- Green: Black-eyed Susan, grass, coneflower heads and petals, lilac flowers, peony flowers, peach leaves, spinach, sage

- Yellow: Goldenrod, mums, celery leaves, chamomile, daffodil flowers (dried), marigolds, red clover (flowers and stems)

Potpourri

Roses are the first flowers we think of when we think of making potpourri, but they aren't the only ones. Other flowers and plants that keep their scent when dried include scented geraniums, lavender, lemon balm, mint, honeysuckle, and lilacs. I'm sure there are others. You will just have to experiment with what you grow.

You can also use blooms that don't smell to make your potpourri look pretty and natural. Some good candidates include red clover heads, rosebuds, tiny carnations (they sometimes smell), baby's breath, gomphrena, statice, and celosia.

The internet will provide you with an abundance of recipes and instructions for making potpourri, so I'll leave it at that and move on.

Crafts

There are many craft projects in which flowers can be used. Most involve flowers that have been dried, but there are a few that call for live specimens. Once again, the types of flowers suitable for each project will vary. If you are unsure of what types of flowers will work for your project, ask someone with experience, experiment, or look it up in a book or online.

Some of the most popular crafts you can make from flowers and vegetables include:

- Dried flower arrangements

- Dried vegetable wreaths

- Pressed flowers used in making bookmarks, wall hangings, and jewelry

  - Example: I read an article about a woman who picked some forsythia, lilac, and sweet peas from the plants growing in her parents' yard while preparing to sell the house to settle the estate. She kept the blossoms alive long enough to have little flowers recreated from their petals and the talents of an artist. The artist arranged them on a small ceramic disc and then encased the disc in gold-rimmed glass and put each of them on a delicate gold chain, creating a necklace for each of her daughters. What a sweet way to preserve a bit of your family's heritage and memories!

Live plant sculptures and wreaths using
- succulents, mosses, or ivies

- Potato ink stamps

- Table arrangements from dried

- corn and grasses Old-fashioned

apple head doll

Edibles and tea

Of course, you know vegetables are edible *and* that you should eat them every day. Most vegetables can be eaten raw or cooked. Some vegetables you cannot eat raw are potatoes and okra. Raw green beans aren't all that great, either, but it isn't forbidden, by any means. You also likely know that herbs are meant for eating.

- Mint, lemon balm, chamomile, and lavender are all great for making tea. You can use the leaves or buds freshly picked or dry them for future use.

- Herbs like cilantro are better fresh than when they are dried. Dill, sage, and rosemary, however, tend to become zestier and more pungent after they are dried. You can use them in sauces, salads, stews, casseroles, soups, and dips.

Did you know there are several types of flowers and leaves that are edible, too? Here are a list of edible flowers and leaves:

- Annise (licorice tasting)
- Apple blossoms (in moderation)
- Small carnations (peppery tasting)
- Chives (you know you can eat the green, but you can eat the purple flowers, too)

- Dandelions (raw flowers taste like pepper, those cooked in butter taste more like mushrooms. The smaller and younger the better.)

Dandelion greens

Honeysuckle (just not the berries, which are toxic)

Impatiens (sweet tasting)

- Lavender buds
- Squash blossoms (raw or batter-fried)
- Rose petals and buds
- Violet petals
- There are several other flowers that are edible. This website is one of many that lists them: https://commonsensehome.com/edible-flowers/

NOTE: Just because it is edible doesn't mean it tastes good. Many flowers and leaves have a bitter or tangy taste—especially those that are fully bloomed. Usually, when it comes to edible flowers, the younger they are, the better they taste.

Medicinal purposes

Before I give you a list of some flowers and plants you can grow that have proven medicinal purposes, I need to make one thing clear. **This list and the information provided are in NO WAY meant to serve as medical advice. I am in NO WAY suggesting you go against your doctor's advice and treatment plan in favor of self-medicating with plants and flowers.** This doesn't mean, however, that these plants are without curative properties. Many medications are plant-based and let's face it—they've been around since the beginning of time and have been used to treat and cure people for centuries. That being said, you should take your whole health into consideration when contemplating using natural medicines and if you have existing conditions, you should always consult with your physician before doing anything that might interfere with your current treatment plan.

Something else I want to pass on is the fact that a lot of medicinal plants are wild plants and trees—not things you would usually grow in your garden. I will not be listing those, as this is a book about gardening—not wildcrafting.

Plants you might put in your garden that have medicinal qualities include:

- Begonia: Drinking water infused with the blooms cures headaches, and gives relief from burns and sores when the leaves and blooms are rubbed on the affected area.

- Butterfly weed: When used in tea and cooked in food, it can ease respiratory problems; it can reduce swelling when used in a poultice. Carnations: Made into a tea, it reduces stress, anxiety, and fatigue.

- Dandelion: The leaves and roots made into a tea cures anemia and increases the overall health of your blood cells.

- Jasmine: Use the flowers to brew a tea that cures digestive problems.

Morning Glory flowers: These can be used as a laxative, but with great care.

- Peony: Using the petals to make an infused water or tea can treat menstrual cramps and muscle cramps.
- Roses: The petals can be eaten to relieve anxiety and boost circulation. Rose petal tea is a mild laxative, and crushed rose petals made into a paste have an amazing smoothing effect on our skin.

The following websites offer more details but remember: this should not be used in place of professional medical advice or treatment.

https://www.proflowers.com/blog/medicinal-flowers-and-uses

http://www.remedieshouse.com/herbs/15-beautiful-flowering-plants-withmedicinal-uses/

https://themysteriousworld.com/top-15-most-powerful-medicinal-plants/

Be honest—when you first started thinking about taking up gardening as a hobby, did you know how many practical applications it could have?

SEVEN

All Good Things Must Come to an End...
Until Next Year

*There are two seasonal diversions
that can ease the bite of any
winter. One is the January thaw.
The other is the seed catalogues.
~Hal Borland*

Whether a plant is a perennial or an annual, it has a lifecycle. If it is an annual, it sprouts from a seed, grows, produces, reaches peak production, slowly decreases its productivity, and then dies off. If the plant is a perennial, it 'wakes up' in the spring and puts on new growth, matures enough to produce, reaches its peak in productivity, and then slows down until it recognizes that it is time to go dormant for the winter. This 'recognition' comes from colder temperatures, shorter days, and less intense sunshine. In either case, even if you live in a climate where it stays warm (or relatively warm) year-round, your plants won't keep producing year-round. They need to rest just like we do.

Preparing your flower bed and garden for winter is not difficult. It is, however, an important part of gardening, because just like you and I sleep better when our environment is conducive to a good night's sleep, so do your plants and so does your soil.

The most (or almost most) important thing to remember is water. I know, I know—by the time mid-August rolls around and your plants are no longer as pretty as they were and you are only getting one or two cucumbers a week instead of six or eight a day, you are ready to call it quits for the year. It's no longer as enjoyable to water your plants because you aren't getting the same benefits as you were before. **You need to keep watering**, because even though the plants don't look like they are benefitting from the moisture, they are. The roots are benefitting from it, using it to become stronger and wellnourished so they can survive the cold (if you live in a cold climate), and to work behind the scenes for the next growing season. Once your plants begin to slow down or stop producing (flowers or food), you still need to make sure they get an inch or two of water on them and the ground around them every week up until the time the ground freezes. At that point you can stop watering until spring.

You also need to **keep your garden weeded, making sure the area(s) are as weed-free as possible by first frost.** Keeping your garden weed-free throughout the dormant period will greatly reduce the amount of weeding you will have to do next year. If there are weeds there, your plants' seeds cannot fall to the ground in your garden area and germinate.

Remove dead annuals. As your annual plants quit producing and die off, pull them up and get rid of them. NOTE: If the plants don't have thick woody stems or stalks, like corn, okra, tomatoes, and zinnias, pull them up by the roots, use your hoe to chop them up, and till or spade them into the soil. In other words, use your plants as compost. The plant matter will add nutrients to the soil, but more than that, it improves the structure of the soil, making it easier for roots to grab hold of.

Cut your perennials. Using your garden shears, you can cut your perennials back to where they are three or four inches above the ground. This includes your iris and daylilies. Afterward, hoe up the ground around the plants to loosen the soil so that any compost you add throughout the winter will be beneficial. This will also work in any seeds that have fallen from plants like coneflowers and dianthus, as well as self-sowing annuals like zinnias, to snuggle down for the winter.

To blanket or not to blanket...

Some gardeners prefer to cover their flowerbeds with a layer of mulched up leaves as a means of blanketing the soil for the winter. They do so in order to protect the perennials and the self-sowing seeds. This isn't necessary. Besides, it creates more work in the spring— you either have to rake the leaves off or work them into the soil.

The steps we've just gone through apply to both in-ground and raised beds. If you are a container gardener, you will need to:

- Pull your plants and get rid of them, but feel free to chop up the leaves and work them into the soil.

- Empty the soil out of all the small pots (12 inches or smaller). Don't get rid of the soil. Put it in some plastic storage bins and store it in your garden shed, basement, or wherever. Don't put the lids on the storage bins. Let it breath and add compost to it throughout the winter.
- For larger pots, work the soil over after you remove the plants and add compost to it periodically throughout the winter.

NOTE: One question novice gardeners always have is whether or not they can reuse potting soil from year to year. The answer is yes, but you need to enrich the soil between growing seasons by adding compost to it.

As you know, the soil is the main supplier of nutrients to a plant. Plants that are in the ground or in raised beds have the benefit of living in soil that is continually being replenished with worm casings, decomposing leaves and grass that feed the ground around the garden, the air and sunshine. This isn't the case with soil in pots. Even though the pots are outside, exposed to sun and rain, it just isn't the same. But when you add compost or fertilize the soil before the next growing season, you can get a few years out of it.

You can also extend the life of your potting soil by mixing it with new potting soil every year or two. The important thing is that you remove it from the smaller pots and turn it well in larger pots to break up any root balls and to enrich it in preparation for the next year.

Following your garden clean-up, all that's left to do is start planning for next year.

EIGHT

What Inquiring Minds Want to Know

I cultivate my garden, and my garden cultivates me. ~Robert Brault

Throughout the pages of this book I've tried to give you a basic, but thorough beginner's guide to the most common and popular gardening methods. The emphasis has been on the mechanics of gardening. Now I want to bring it all together by answering the questions people tend to ask once they decide to try their hand at gardening. Some of the answers may be repetitions of things you have already read, but that's okay. If it's important enough to put in here twice, it's important enough to read it twice. So, without further ado...

Q: What are the most forgiving or fail-proof plants to grow?

A: There are several that fall into this category. NOTE: These are not listed in order of importance or fool-proofness.

*Asparagus is started from roots of the plants. It needs to be planted somewhere it can be left alone and undisturbed. Along a fence row, designating one end of your garden as an asparagus bed, or devoting an entire raised bed for this delicious vegetable will be best. Once it is planted, all you have to do is wait for it to grow (early to late spring). Asparagus self-seeds, but it usually takes two to four years for you to realize a harvest. It is well worth the wait, so don't get discouraged.

Q: Is it better to start from seed or seedling plants?

A: Most of the time you will do better if you start your flowers with seedling plants. The main reason for this is that flowers take much longer to mature than vegetables. The exception to this is zinnias and sunflowers. You will also find that planting iris and lilies using just the chromes will work just fine, too.

When it comes to vegetables, however, it is almost always better to start from seed, with the exception of tomatoes, which need to be started indoors if you want to enjoy the fruits of your labor before the growing season is over.

Q: Is there anything to the old sayings about planting according to the signs of the moon and other such things?

A: Yes, most definitely! For example, a new moon pulls water up from the ground, which in turn, swells a seed and causes it to burst open (germinate). That is why planting within a day or two of the new moon causes quick productivity.

Here is a great website that explains it in more detail. And trust me, you'll do well to take heed.

https://itsgreenday.blogspot.com/2009/04/how-moon-affects-plantgrowth.html

Q: What's the difference between garden soil and potting soil?

A: Potting soil is less dense. It contains little or no actual dirt/soil, but is a combination of peat moss, vermiculite or perlite, sand, and even finely ground tree bark. Potting soil has also undergone a sterilization process to kill any weeds and seeds that would interfere with plant growth. Garden soil contains actual soil, so it is much denser and doesn't drain as well as potting soil, and it tends to get packed down in pots.

Q: What about succulents? Are they easy to grow?

A: Yes. Succulents, which include cactus, are very easy to grow. They require next to no care and prefer not to be watered very often. In fact, I know people who have beautiful cacti that grow well with only a tiny bit of water every month or so. There are so many varieties of succulents to choose from, you can have a diverse and attractive display with very little work on your part. NOTE: Succulents do best in containers in most parts of the country.

Q: Are berries easy to grow, and can they be grown in small areas?

A: Strawberries are very easy to grow and can be grown in an area as small as 5x5 feet. Strawberry plants are a lot like bunnies—they multiply rapidly. You will need to thin your plants out each spring before they begin to bloom. You do this by simply pulling some of the plants out of the ground. You will also have to break their runners to separate them from their 'parent' plant. Sell or give your excess plants to someone. Blackberries, blueberries, raspberries, and all other berries require a lot more room and attention.

Q: Is one kind of mulch better than another?

A: Mulch is a matter of opinion. When you think of mulch, you tend to think in terms of cypress, cedar, or pine wood chunks. But there are actually several other materials you can use for mulch. They include rubber, pea gravel, creek gravel, nut hulls, cocoa bean hulls, and lava rock. Deciding what you use to mulch your gardens (if you use anything at all) depends on a number of things. For example, if your garden consists primarily of perennials, or if you have an area of your yard designated for pots, rock is often your best option. It doesn't have to be replaced, it doesn't attract insects (like wood does), and it requires next to no maintenance. Vegetable gardens or flower beds you will be tilling or spading every season don't need mulch. And finally, be sure your pets won't ingest the nut hulls, cocoa bean hulls, or rubber, as all are toxic to them.

Q: What are community gardens?

A: Community gardens are gardens used and tended to by several individuals. Most community gardens rent space to people to use for growing vegetables and herbs. Each person is responsible for keeping their own area of the garden weeded, watered, and tended to. I'll be honest—I don't know how community gardens keep people from taking things that aren't theirs. I assume it's based on an honor system, which *should* work. If you participate in a community garden venture, you still need to have your own tools, fertilizer, pest prevention, and so forth. Community gardens can be a great way to enjoy raising your own herbs and vegetables as long as you don't get tired of traveling back and forth to take care of your space.

Q: How do I know what planting zone I'm in?

A: This map shows the different planting zones in the United States.

Q: What flowers attract hummingbirds and butterflies?

A: Impatiens, petunias, hollyhocks, honeysuckle, bee balm, columbine, lilies, and phlox are a few of the most popular hummingbird attractants. Hibiscus, coneflowers, butterfly bush, sunflowers, lilac, zinnias, sweet william, petunias, and dianthus are just a few of the many flowers that will bring butterflies to your garden.

Q: Is it better to overwater or underwater your plants?

A: Neither. You need to make sure your plants get the amount of water they need AND that their home (ground, raised bed, or container) has proper drainage. When your plant is getting too much water, leaves will become pale and yellow and the plant will look limp. If they aren't getting enough water, leaves will drop in an effort to conserve food and energy for the main part of the plant.

Q: I see all sorts of unconventional things being used as flower or vegetable containers. What special preparation, if any, needs to be done to use these things?

A: Using 'unconventional' items to pot plants and flowers in is a great way to add a bit of whimsy and personal flair to your landscape. Flowers and plants look fine in traditional pots, but they look spectacular in an old suitcase, a cowboy boot, a vintage child's dump truck or lunch box, a dresser no longer in good enough condition to hold clothes, or whatever else appeals to you. The only preparation you need to make is to ensure the container has adequate drainage, so plants don't become waterlogged.

FYI: Other unusual items you can use for your container garden include:

Old tins

Purses

- Wheelbarrow
- Baskets
- Old tires
- Wooden boxes
- These websites also contain a lot of good ideas:

- https://balconygardenweb.com/planter-ideas-from-household-items/
- https://www.pinterest.com/provenwinners/unusual-gardencontainers/

Q: What things are compostable?

A: The most compostable materials are:

- Vegetable peelings
- Leaves
- Straw
- Sawdust
- Pine needles
- Small sticks

Bark

- Paper towel and toilet paper tubes
- Newsprint (not glossy)
- Dryer lint
- Egg shells
- Coffee grounds
- Dead plants
- Stale bread, crackers, cereal
- Burlap

L
iv
es
to
ck
m
an
ur
e

Q:

W

ha

t

th

in

gs

ca

n'

t I

co

m

p

os

t?

A: You cannot compost:

Diseased plants

Meat, pasta, bones

- Synthetics
- Walnut hull, leaves, and twigs
- Pet manure
- Human waste
- Plastic
- Glossy paper
- Dairy products

Q: How do I know if my soil is too acidic?

A: You can have a professional soil test done without spending a lot of money. You can also do it yourself using nothing more than a sealable clear glass jar, soil from your garden, and water. To test your soil, fill the jar about half full of soil from the garden you want to test. Fill the jar the rest of the way with water, leaving about an inch of space at the top. Seal the jar and shake it vigorously. Let it set untouched for 24 hours. During this time the soil will separate into layers of silt, clay, and sand.

The bottom layer is heavier particles of sand and rocks. The layer on top of sand is silt. Clay particles are the top layer. The ideal soil will be approximately 20% clay, 40% silt, and 40% sand and loam mixture. You also need to notice the color or tint of your soil. The lighter the soil's color, the less organic matter it contains. If this is the case with your soil, you need to add compost matter to it to help your plants grow.

NINE

Resources for Gardeners

Seeds

Harris seeds:
https://www.harrisseeds.com/?
msclkid=b4d56264cf17117d07023e916ffb49ff&
utm_source=bing&utm_medi
%20TM%20-%20Bing%20-%20HS%20-
%20Harris%20Seeds&utm_term=Harris%20Seed
s&utm_content=Harris%20S

Burpee:
https://www.burpee.com/homepage?
cid=PPC&msclkid=87fd3805f5f71e1926fa64f054
e5b225

Gurney's:
https://www.gurneys.com/category/best_seeds
_of_gurneys/a?
p=0564989&msclkid=26de3a9985ad151691796
66c2483ab66&utm_source=b

Baker
seed:
https://w

ww.rares
eeds.co
m/

Garden tools

Your local farm and home store, big box discount stores like Wal-Mart, and home stores like Lowes, Menards, and Home Depot are all great sources for garden tools.

Mulch

Local garden centers are your best option for mulch and border materials. NOTE: If you are going to be doing an area larger than 8x8 feet, it will be much more cost-effective to buy your mulch in bulk rather than by the bag.

Potting soil

Miracle Gro, Black Gold, and Epsoma are by far the best brands of potting soil. This isn't to say other brands won't do the trick, but I strongly suggest you stay away from off-brands or store brands. When it comes to potting soil, you get what you pay for.

Compost and fertilizer

Composting doesn't have to be complicated. It is a natural process of putting plant and food matter together to rot so that it can be used as fertilizer for the soil. It requires very little input on your part. All you need to do is designate an area for your compost and then do one of the following:

- Build a composting box (bottomless) out of lumber, chain link fencing, or chicken wire stretched across a 2x4 frame.

- Keep a compost bucket in your kitchen for all food-related compostable items. At the end of the day, bury the bucket's contents in your designated composting area using a small shovel.

If you choose to put your compost in a composting box:

- Begin with a thick layer of dead leaves and lawn clippings.

Dump your compostable garbage into the box.

Turn the compost with a pitchfork, doing your best to bury the fresh compost so as not to attract unwanted visitors to your yard (raccoons, possums, etc).

Add moisture to your compost to aid in decomposition.

- Use the compost from the bottom of the
- pile first.

If you choose to bury your compost:

- Dig a small hole to bury each day's
- refuse.

- Work in one direction so you don't dig in the same exact spot.

After a period of a few weeks, you can begin using the composted soil in your garden area.

The purpose of compost is to fertilize your soil, but if you want or need more than your composting efforts can provide, fertilizer can be purchased anywhere plant supplies are sold.

Local help and information

The content of this book, as well as most gardening books, is somewhat generic. It doesn't cover the specifics of your location and the general soil content of your area. It would be impossible to cover all these bases. That's what farm service agents, county extension agents, master gardener groups, and locally owned garden centers and greenhouse businesses are for. These folks know what works and what doesn't for your area. They know what pests and plant diseases you might have to deal with AND how best to deal with them. Get to know these people and let them help you establish and maintain a healthy, beautiful, and bountiful garden.

What better way to end this book than with some inspirational and encouraging thoughts on what gardening can do for you?

I think this is what hooks one to gardening: it is the closest one can come to being present at creation. ~Phyllis Theroux

If you've never experienced the joy of accomplishing more than you can imagine, plant a garden. ~Robert Brault

Earth is here so kind, that just tickle her with a hoe and she laughs with a harvest. ~Douglas William Jerrold, about Australia

A house without a garden or orchard is unfurnished and incomplete. ~A. Bronson Alcott

Gardens are a form of autobiography. ~Sydney Eddison

CPSIA information can be obtained
at www.ICGtesting.com
Printed in the USA
BVHW061311030621
608733BV00012B/3589